THE 12-WEEK
CANNABIS
REDUCTION
JOURNEY

NICHOLE SLOAN

Contents

Welcome!

I want to commend you for the bravery and self-love it took to take this step towards your own healing. You holding this book shows that you are braver than you know and you are ready to begin. You are standing at the threshold of change, even if part of you is unsure.

For many, cannabis has been a source of comfort and a close friend—something that eased pain, softened stress, or provided relief when nothing else did. But there often comes a point when what once soothed begins to take more than it gives. Energy feels lower, joy feels muted, and the habit feels stronger than choice.

This book is here to walk beside you as you explore a new way forward. May this book be more than just a plan, but a companion—offering a weaving of science, compassion, and spirit. You will find practical tools here, but also reminders that you are not broken, you are not failing—you are remembering your wholeness. One day at a time.

If at any point you forget why you started, return to these truths:

You are worthy. You are capable. You are evolving. You deserve to come home to yourself.

May you meet yourself with compassion and ease,

Introduction

A Healing Journey — A Path to Balance, Healing, and Renewal

You are standing at the threshold of a sacred return — not to the person you were before, but to the deeper self that has always been calling to you from beneath the surface of habit, pain, or forgetfulness.

This 12-week journey is not simply about releasing cannabis. It is an invitation into greater **balance**, **wholeness**, and healing — one rooted in science, nourished by spirit, and guided by your own inner wisdom. Each week, you will step further into alignment with your true nature, weaving together the neurobiology of healing with daily practices that tend the body, soothe the nervous system, awaken your energy, and restore your sense of purpose.

What This Journey Offers You:

- **Cannabis Reduction with Intention:** A clear, gentle framework to taper cannabis use while honoring your body's rhythm and unique needs.

- **Dopamine and Neurotransmitter Renewal:** Support for the brain's natural motivation and reward systems to reawaken joy and energy.

- **Endocannabinoid System Rebalancing:** Practices and nourishment that restore your body's own cannabinoid harmony.

- **Spiritual Integration:** Tools to reconnect with your higher self, intuition, and the divine intelligence within your body and breath.

- **Somatic and Cognitive Fear Reduction:** Techniques to regulate and soothe the nervous system and rewire limiting beliefs.

- **Community and Connection:** Invitations to return to relational wholeness — with others, with the Earth, and with yourself.

- **Dietary and Supplement Support:** Foods and natural compounds that nourish the brain, calm the nervous system, and promote clarity.

- **Weekly Mantras and Spiritual Practices:** Use of spirituality to guide your intention, elevate your vibration, and call in your deepest healing.

How the Path Unfolds:

Each week of this journey offers a unique focus — a doorway into one dimension of healing. These weekly rhythms flow like seasons, spiraling through layers of body, brain, emotion, and spirit:

- **Weeks 1–4**: Foundation & Stabilization — Gentle cannabis reduction, nervous system soothing, basic brain nutrition, and grounding in supportive practices.

- **Weeks 5–8**: Regeneration & Renewal — Dopamine recalibration, emotional release, spiritual re-connection, and deeper integration of identity without cannabis.

- **Weeks 9–12**: Empowerment & Expansion — Creating your best life, community reconnection, embodiment of your healed self, and long-term self-healing.

You are not walking alone. Your brain, body, and soul are ready. And I am here — a voice of compassionate reflection and steady companionship — to support your every step.

Before You Begin

Pause. Breathe. Place a hand on your heart or belly.

Whisper to yourself: *"I am ready to return to balance. I trust in my ability to heal."*

There is no rush. There is no failure. There is only presence, process, and the sacred remembering of who you are.

Welcome home.

Compassionate Reflection

Getting Started

- How does it feel to think about letting go or reducing your cannabis intake? What emotions come to the surface? What fears are present?

- Remember it is healthy and to be expected to feel fear as you embark on any journey. Courage is not the absence of fear, it is action in the face of it.

- What words of encouragement or compassion can you offer yourself as you begin?

Ex. I'm scared of stopping. It helps my anxiety so much I don't know how I'll manage if I stop. But I know I've quit things before and I remember that it's a process, that gets easier over time. I can remind myself that I am powerful and capable and I get to reduce slowly, this won't be overnight.

_____

_____

_____

_____

_____

_____

_____

_____

_____

_____

The Crossroads

Choosing to Quit or Reduce

There comes a moment in every healing journey when you reach a fork in the path. One trail is shaded and quiet—it leads to gradual release, a gentle tapering of what no longer serves. The other shines with clarity and stillness—it leads to complete letting go. Both are sacred. Both are available to you. And only your heart can choose which trail is yours.

This is not a test of strength. It is not a question of willpower or morality. It is a question of alignment. Of rhythm. Of readiness.

To reduce is to say:

"I am not ready to leave this behind completely, but I want to shift our relationship. I want to remember who I am without relying on it so often."

This path honors pacing. It can feel more gentle, more sustainable for some. It allows you to observe your patterns with curiosity and compassion. It teaches moderation, presence, and the subtle art of choice.

To quit completely is to say:

"This chapter is finished. I am ready to release this fully, and trust that what I truly need is already within me."

This path is clear and bold. It may come after many cycles of trial. It brings a kind of sacred cleansing—a breaking of old patterns. It creates space, instantly, for the new to bloom.

How do you know which path is right for you?

Ask yourself not from your mind, but from your body.

- How does your chest feel when you imagine being free from cannabis?

- How does your breath move when you consider a slow reduction?

- What words or images appear when you whisper to yourself, *"What do I truly need now?"*

Sometimes, reduction is the right medicine. Sometimes, freedom only comes when the cord is cut. And sometimes, you begin on one trail and later find yourself guided to the other.

There is no wrong way. Only your way.

And no matter the path, your garden will bloom in response to your honesty. With every step, the soil becomes richer, the roots more certain, and the light more welcoming.

You are already on the journey.

And you are already enough.

Compassionate Reflection

Abstinence vs. Reduction

- What has your intuition told you about your cannabis use?

- What led you to this workbook?

- What do you hope to gain from this process; a reduction or complete abstinence?

- You don't have to know how you'll get there; the first step is simply identifying the goal and planting the seed.

Ex. I'm ready to reduce slowly. I've tried stopping abruptly before and I felt so uncomfortable. I want to give my body time to adjust to less cannabis in my system. I came to the workbook to find tools to supplement my smoking. My ultimate goal is to reduce, but if that feels good to my mind and body I'd consider stopping altogether.

_____

_____

_____

_____

_____

_____

_____

_____

_____

_____

The Benefits of Tapering versus Abstinence

The Benefits of Tapering Cannabis Use in Healing Cannabis Use Disorder

Gradual reduction, or tapering, of cannabis use is increasingly recognized as an effective approach for individuals seeking to heal from cannabis use disorder. Unlike abrupt cessation, tapering allows the brain and nervous system to adjust more slowly, which can reduce withdrawal symptoms and improve the chances of sustained recovery.

When cannabis use has been regular and long-term, the endocannabinoid system and related neural pathways adapt to its presence. Suddenly stopping cannabis can trigger significant physiological and psychological withdrawal symptoms, including anxiety, irritability, sleep disturbances, and mood instability. These symptoms often contribute to relapse and discomfort.

Tapering cannabis use provides a more gradual decrease in THC exposure, enabling the endocannabinoid system to recalibrate without causing excessive stress to the nervous system. This method supports neurochemical balance by allowing dopamine and other neurotransmitter systems to adjust incrementally, which may reduce the intensity of withdrawal symptoms.

Tapering also helps maintain motivation and emotional regulation during recovery, which are critical for long-term success. By minimizing abrupt neurochemical shifts, tapering can stabilize mood and cognitive function.

In summary, tapering cannabis use:

- Reduces the severity of withdrawal symptoms

- Supports neurochemical and nervous system recalibration

- Improves emotional and motivational stability

- Enhances the likelihood of sustained recovery

This approach is considered both safer and more effective for many individuals, especially those with co-occurring mental health conditions or nervous system dysregulation.

THC & CBD Then vs. Now

Why Today's Cannabis Raises the Risk of Cannabis Use Disorder

Modern cannabis carries a far greater risk of dependence than past decades because of its high THC levels and low CBD content. Higher potency means the brain is exposed to much larger doses of THC per use, which speeds up the cycle of tolerance, withdrawal, and craving. At the same time, the natural buffering effect of CBD is mostly absent, leaving THC's impact unmoderated. This combination increases the likelihood of developing Cannabis Use Disorder (CUD)—a condition marked by compulsive use despite harm, difficulty cutting back, and withdrawal symptoms such as irritability, sleep disturbance, and anxiety. Studies consistently show that people who use high-potency products daily face the highest risk, especially adolescents and young adults whose brains are still developing.

THC & CBD Then vs. Now:

Then (1970s–1990s)

- THC levels: ~1–4%

- CBD: present in higher proportion

- THC:CBD ratio: ~14:1 (balanced by today's standards)

- User experience: milder "high," less risk of paranoia or dependence

Now (2000s–2020s)

- THC levels: 15–23% in flower, 60–90% in concentrates

- CBD: often <0.15% or missing

- THC:CBD ratio: ~80:1

- User experience: more intense intoxication, higher tolerance, more withdrawal symptoms, greater risk of Cannabis Use Disorder (CUD)

Why It Matters

- CBD buffers THC: Less CBD = more chance of anxiety, paranoia, or agitation.

- Potency drives risk: Higher THC is linked to higher odds of dependence.

- Frequency multiplies risk: Daily high-THC use accelerates tolerance and withdrawal.

- Youth vulnerability: Developing brains (under 25) are more affected.

Key Numbers at a Glance

- 1970s: <2% THC

- 1995: ~4% THC

- 2014: ~12% THC

- 2022: ~16% THC

- Today's retail: Flower ~18–23% THC; Concentrates 60–90% THC

Cannabis Withdrawal Symptoms

How to Cope During Withdrawal

Cannabis withdrawal is real — and for many, it's the hardest part of the healing journey. While often downplayed or misunderstood, withdrawal is not a sign of weakness or failure. It is the body and brain adjusting to life without a substance that once provided comfort, relief, and regulation.

The most important truth: withdrawal is temporary. Compassion, patience, and preparation can transform this uncomfortable phase into an opportunity for deep healing.

Common Cannabis Withdrawal Symptoms

Not everyone will experience all of these, but many notice a mix. Symptoms usually begin within 24–72 hours after reducing or stopping use and can last 1–2 weeks, sometimes longer for sleep or mood changes.

- Sleep disturbance: difficulty falling asleep, vivid dreams, night sweats

- Mood changes: irritability, sadness, anxiety, restlessness

- Physical discomfort: headaches, sweating, chills, appetite changes

- Cognitive effects: brain fog, trouble focusing, forgetfulness

- Cravings: strong urges to return to cannabis, especially in familiar routines

In compassion-based recovery, we don't ask, "Why am I suffering like this?"

We ask, "What does my body need to feel safe again?"

Withdrawal is your nervous system asking for support while it recalibrates. The 12-week cannabis reduction journey is the medicine that carries you through.

Practical Coping Strategies

1. Sleep Disturbances

- Gentle evening ritual: dim lights, herbal tea (chamomile, lemon balm), magnesium supplement

- Breath practice: 4-7-8 breathing to activate parasympathetic calm

- Reframe vivid dreams: remind yourself they are the brain's way of "detoxing" stored experiences

2. Mood Shifts (Anxiety, Irritability, Sadness)

- Grounding tools: 5-4-3-2-1 sensory check-in when anxiety spikes

- Movement medicine: walking, yoga, dancing release natural endorphins

- Self-talk mantra: "This feeling is temporary. I am safe in my healing."

3. Physical Discomfort

- Hydration: drink water with electrolytes to flush the system

- Nutrition: omega-3 rich foods (chia, walnuts, salmon) to stabilize endocannabinoid receptors

- Gentle stretching: to ease tension and headaches

4. Cognitive Fog

- Single-tasking: focus on one activity at a time to reduce overwhelm

- Micro-breaks: 5 minutes of sunlight, deep breathing, or music every 2 hours

- Patience: cognitive clarity returns gradually as the brain rebalances

5. Cravings

- Delay technique: tell yourself, "I can wait 10 minutes." Urges often pass in waves.

- Replacement ritual: tea, candle, or soothing activity at your usual use time

- Support person: text a trusted friend when cravings peak

The Role of Self-Compassion

The hardest withdrawal symptom isn't headaches or insomnia — it's the inner critic that says: "You can't do this. You're weak. You're failing."

The antidote is compassionate self-talk:

- "This discomfort means my body is healing."

- "I am strong enough to stay the course."

- "I deserve peace and clarity.

Withdrawal is not a punishment; it's a passage. Each symptom is your body learning how to self-regulate again. By meeting this phase with compassion, patience, and supportive practices, you transform it from an obstacle into a teacher.

Remember: You are not alone. Every breath you take without cannabis is a step toward freedom, clarity, and self-trust.

Why 12 Weeks?

Embracing Time as a Healing Ally

Healing is a process, not a race. Twelve weeks offers a sacred container—long enough to gently retrain your body and mind, yet focused enough to hold your intention clearly.

In this reduction journey, your nervous system has space to recalibrate without overwhelm. Neurotransmitters like dopamine and endocannabinoids can gradually find their new balance, reducing symptoms of withdrawal. Neural pathways that once relied on cannabis support can begin to forge fresh, resilient connections.

This timeframe honors the complexity of change. It acknowledges that withdrawal symptoms and emotional waves may ebb and flow. It gives you permission to move at your own pace, cultivating patience and self-compassion.

Twelve weeks also allows for layering new habits—spiritual practices, movement, community, nourishing diet—to take root and flourish alongside your taper. It becomes not just about letting go, but about creating a vibrant, sustainable foundation for your well-being.

In this way, 12 weeks isn't just a countdown—it's a journey of transformation, a powerful invitation to witness your strength and renewal with kindness.

Tending the Inner Garden

Cultivating Motivation for Change

Before any great transformation, there is a quiet moment of looking inward—like standing at the edge of a garden that's overgrown, wild with habits, and ready for something new. Motivation doesn't always arrive with a roar. Sometimes it's a whisper: *There's more for me than this. I'm ready to remember who I am beneath the weeds.*

Motivation, like a seed, needs the right conditions to take root:

- **Readiness** is the loosened soil.

- **Hope** is the sunlight.

- **Support** is the rain.

In early change, it's normal to feel uncertain or tired. You may long for new growth while still craving the old shelter. This is not a failure—it's the natural tension of transition. In fact, ambivalence is often the first green shoot breaking through.

You don't need to be fully confident. You only need willingness.

Try asking yourself gently:

- *What is quietly calling for my attention and compassion?*

- *What part of me is beginning to grow, even if I don't see it yet?*

- *What compassionate self talk do I need to help this change feel possible?*

Change begins not with pressure, but with presence. By noticing your inner garden—without judgment—you become the kind gardener of your own healing. One small act of tending at a time, and something new will bloom.

Compassionate Reflection

The "WHY"

- How does it feel to embark on a new journey?

- WHY did you use cannabis regularly? What were it's benefits?

  The benefits you experienced from cannabis can be your new goal in recovery. For example, if you used cannabis to relieve anxiety, the new goal can be to find ways to manage anxiety and relax the nervous system.

- All thoughts and emotions are welcome here.

Ex. I'm so nervous to stop smoking because of my anxiety. But, I've never done activities to regulate my nervous system and I've definitely never changed my diet to promote brain health! So, it's worthwhile for me to try something new and see if I can manage my anxiety naturally without cannabis.

_____

_____

_____

_____

_____

_____

_____

_____

_____

_____

Saying Goodbye

Changing Your Relationship with Cannabis

Find your quiet place. This can be indoors or outside—in your garden, beneath a favorite tree, or a peaceful corner where you feel safe.

Gather simple tools if you like:

- A journal or paper

- A pen

- A small candle or a bowl of water (something to symbolize release)

Step 1: Ground Yourself

Close your eyes. Take three deep, slow breaths. Feel your feet rooted like the roots of a tree, grounding you to the Earth. Let your shoulders soften. Invite presence.

Step 2: Speak to Your Old Friend

In your journal or aloud, speak to cannabis as you would to a cherished companion. You might say:

"Thank you for the times you held me. For the shelter, the comfort, the relief. Thank you for always being there for me"

Acknowledge what it has meant to you, both the light and the shadow.

Step 3: Express Your Grief and Gratitude

Write or say:

"I feel sadness letting you go, because you were once so important." "I am grateful for the ways you helped me, even if now it's time to walk a different path."

Step 4: Declare Your Intention

State clearly what you are choosing now: *"I am ready to change our relationship." "I am choosing to reduce/quit so I can discover who I am without you." "I honor you and release you with love."*

Step 5: Symbolic Release

If you have a candle, light it and imagine the flame transforming your old patterns into light. If you have water, you might gently splash or sprinkle it as a symbol of cleansing and renewal. Or simply visualize letting go—watch leaves flowing down a river, or a balloon gently reaching towards the sky.

Step 6: Close with Compassion

Place your hand over your heart and say:

"I am gentle with myself as I walk this path." "I trust my inner wisdom to guide me." "I am open to new growth, one step at a time."

Compassionate Reflection

Saying Goodbye

- Cannabis may be one of the longest relationships of your life. Letting go and saying goodbye will feel similar to a breakup. Honor the tenderness that is present, the fear, and possibly the relief. Allow space for all of it to be present in this moment.

- Write your goodbye letter to cannabis below.

_____

_____

_____

_____

_____

_____

_____

_____

_____

_____

_____

_____

_____

_____

_____

_____

_____

_____

The Grieving Tree

Honoring the Process of Grief

There's a tree in your inner garden—old, strong, familiar. Its branches once offered shade in your loneliest seasons. Its leaves whispered comfort when the world felt too loud. You leaned against it in the quiet, took refuge beneath it in the storms. This tree is your relationship with cannabis.

And now, something inside you knows it's time to change that relationship. To step back. To say goodbye. To let go—not in anger, but in reverence.

This is not just a habit you're releasing. It is a companion. A ritual. A rhythm that cradled you for years. And so, as with any goodbye that matters, **grief will come**.

It may arrive as sadness in your chest. As longing in your hands. As tears that appear out of nowhere. As a strange emptiness at night, when your old friend doesn't arrive to sit beside you.

Let this grief come. Let it speak.

Because grief, when witnessed gently, becomes a kind of gardener too. It loosens the soil around your roots so something new can take hold.

You can thank cannabis for what it gave you. You can name the comfort, the ease, the creativity, the softening. You can bow in gratitude. And then, you can whisper, *"I'm walking a different path now. But you were good to me, when I needed you most."*

This is not weakness. It is not failure.

It is **evolution.**

And even as you let go, the space left behind will not remain empty for long. Already, something new is reaching toward the light. Already, your inner garden is reshaping itself around your truest needs. Already, you are becoming your own sacred shelter.

So let yourself grieve. Let yourself remember. And let yourself begin, again.

The Neurobiology of Healing

Your Brain's Sacred Symphony

Cannabis affects multiple regions of the brain, which is why abrupt cessation can be so uncomfortable for many. In this chapter, we will learn about the different areas of the brain impacted by cannabis and how to work with the brain, not against it.

Healing from cannabis is a sacred journey through the inner landscape of your brain — a living ecosystem where spirit, body, and mind harmonize. This chapter invites you to meet your brain's key regions and systems, to honor their unique roles, and their awaken the ancient wisdom. Together, they form the foundation of your healing journey — a neurological symphony, where each system is an instrument, playing its essential part in your return to wholeness.

The Prefrontal Cortex — The Firekeeper of Consciousness

Nestled behind your forehead, the **prefrontal cortex** is the firekeeper tending the embers of your consciousness. It holds the sacred flame of intention, discernment, and self-mastery. Like a vigilant guardian watching over you, it guides decisions, controls impulses, and tempers emotion with wisdom. When cannabis dims the firekeeper's light, decision-making falters, attention wanes, and cravings can take the reins. Your healing invites this sacred sentinel back into balance.

Scientific Insight:

The prefrontal cortex, particularly the dorsolateral and ventrome-dial regions, is responsible for executive functioning — planning, prioritizing, focusing attention, and regulating emotions and behaviors. Dopamine acts like fuel here, enhancing motivation and cognitive clarity. Chronic cannabis use may reduce dopamine receptor availability, especially in this region, leading to difficulties in sustained attention and inhibition of compulsive urges.

Healing Invitation:

As the firekeeper, your prefrontal cortex is rekindled through:

- **Tyrosine-rich foods** (like eggs, almonds, poultry, and fish)

- **Structured goal-setting**

- **Mindful breathing, mindful meditation and gratitude journaling**

These practices fan the flames of clarity and willpower. Each time you choose presence over impulse, you fortify this sacred fire, allowing this firekeeper to burn bright and guide your path.

The Amygdala — The Emotional Guardian

Deep within your brain's ancient temple, the **amygdala** burns as a watchful flame. This emotional guardian monitors your inner and outer world for threat, sounding the alarm when danger stirs. During withdrawal or emotional upheaval, the amygdala can flare into hypervigilance — stoking anxiety, irritability, and restlessness.

Scientific Insight:

The amygdala is part of the limbic system and plays a key role in emotional learning, fear conditioning, and activation of the **hypothalamic-pituitary-adrenal (HPA) axis**. It stimulates cortisol release through the adrenal glands, contributing to heightened stress responses. Cannabis can dampen this reactivity temporarily, but in its absence, underlying stress circuits may surge unbuffered.

Healing Invitation:

To cool the watchful flame:

- Practice **slow exhalations and vagus nerve toning** (e.g., humming, singing, chanting)

- Engage in **somatic grounding**, such as placing your hands on your heart or belly

- Use affirmations like: *"I am safe in this moment. I belong to the Earth."*

Each act of self-soothing is like rain on the fire's edge, calming the flicker of fear and restoring inner peace.

The Endocannabinoid System & Hippocampus — The Keepers of Balance

Flowing through the depths of your nervous system, the **endo-cannabinoid system (ECS)** is a subtle intelligence, maintaining homeostasis across body and brain. Alongside it flows the **hippocampus**, the scribe of memory and emotion. Together, they weave patterns of balance, repair, and integration. In the wake of cannabis use, this system can become sluggish or overstimulated, and your healing is a sacred call to restore its steady functioning.

Scientific Insight:

The ECS includes **CB1 and CB2 receptors**, endogenous ligands like **anandamide** (the "bliss molecule") and **2-AG**, and enzymes like **FAAH** that degrade cannabinoids. These components regulate neurotransmitter release, immune function, inflammation, sleep, appetite, and mood. THC mimics anandamide, but overuse can desensitize or downregulate CB1 receptors. The **hippocampus**, densely populated with CB1 receptors, is vital for emotional memory, learning, and stress regulation — and is especially sensitive to cannabis-related changes.

Healing Invitation:

Support the ECS by:

- Eating **omega-3-rich foods** (flax, chia, walnuts, wild salmon)

- Practicing **yoga nidra or gentle flow yoga**

- Spending time in **natural environments**, especially near water

- Using essential oils like **lavender** or **frankincense** to support ECS tone

When you honor your body's ability to return to balance, you reactivate sacred inner healing.

Dopamine & Motivation — The Breath of Renewal

The **dopamine system** brings clarity, inspiration, and the breath of renewal. It urges you forward with anticipation, fuels creativity, and helps transform intention into action. After cannabis use, this system can feel grounded, heavy, its spark dimmed. But through healing, it renews again.

Scientific Insight:

Key dopamine pathways — the **mesolimbic (reward)** and **mesocortical (motivation/executive)** circuits — link the **ventral tegmental area (VTA)**, **nucleus accumbens**, and **prefrontal cortex**. Dopamine levels influence mood, drive, and pleasure.

Chronic cannabis use can dysregulate these circuits, reducing the brain's natural response to everyday joys (a condition called **anhedonia**) and making motivation difficult during withdrawal.

Healing Invitation:

To awaken dopamine:

- Engage in **creative play and novelty** (painting, dancing, learning)

- Do **high-intensity interval training (HIIT)** or brisk walks

- Seek **meaningful connection**, laughter, and positive feedback loops

- Eat **protein-rich foods** with B vitamins (spinach, lentils, avocado)

Mantra: *"I breathe in clarity, I move forward with joy."* Let this wind lift your spirit toward vibrant purpose.

The Healing Dance: Weaving Your Brain's Symphony

Picture your inner world as a sacred dance of your four guides:

- **The Firekeeper (prefrontal cortex)** holds the torch of wisdom, tending your vision and values.

- **The Emotional Guardian (amygdala)** burns with fierce love, alert to danger and soothed by presence.

- **The Keepers of Balance (ECS & hippocampus)** maintains balance beneath your awareness, restoring equilibrium and depth.

- **The Breath of Renewal (dopamine system)** breathes through you, inspiring you with joy, curiosity, and movement.

They are not in opposition but in constant interplay — a rhythmic, improvisational healing. When one grows weary, another offers strength. When one flares, another soothes.

Your journey is not about controlling the dance, but listening to it. Honoring the tempo. Surrendering to its intelligence. Your brain is not broken — it is responsive, adaptive, and wise.

Sacred Practices to Support the Whole Symphony

1. **Morning Breathwork**: Begin the day with 5 minutes of extended exhale breathing to calm the amygdala and orient the firekeeper.

2. **Midday Movement**: Walk, dance, or stretch to stimulate dopamine and ECS function.

3. **Evening Reflection**: Write three things you did well today — this lights up the prefrontal cortex and encourages dopamine flow.

4. **Weekly Spirituality**: Return to nature. Sit near water. Light a candle. Speak to your inner allies. Thank them for their labor on your behalf.

You are not alone in this process. These sacred systems are with you, always. They speak through sensation, image, intuition, and breath. You are their steward — the healer returning home, one cell, one thought, one sacred breath at a time.

Cravings Toolkit

Tools to Navigate Restlessness and Longing

Cravings are natural and to be expected in early recovery — cravings are signals from your body and mind to go back to old familiar patterns. We can learn from our cravings; they are not enemies to fight but messages to listen to. This toolkit offers practical and soulful strategies to help you meet cravings with kindness, awareness, and empowered choice.

1. Grounding Practices

- **5-4-3-2-1 Sensory Check:** Name 5 things you see, 4 things you hear, 3 things you feel, 2 things you smell, and 1 thing you taste. This brings you into present moment awareness.

- **Barefoot walking in nature:** Connect your feet with the earth to calm your nervous system and rebalance energy.

- **Self-massage or gentle tapping (EFT):** Stimulate acupressure points to soothe stress and ease cravings.

2. Breath & Body

- **Extended exhale breathing:** Inhale for 4 counts, exhale for 6-8 counts. Repeat 5 times to activate the parasympathetic nervous system.

- **Movement breaks:** Dance, stretch, or do a quick walk to shift energy and reset your mood.

3. Mindful Awareness

- **Name the craving:** "This is a craving, not a command."

- **Remind yourself of your "WHY"-** Why am I engaged in this journey, what are my goals?

- **Journal or voice record:** What emotions or thoughts are beneath this urge? What need is calling for attention?

- **Delay & redirect:** Give yourself 10 minutes before deciding. Often cravings pass like clouds. This skill is called "urge surfing".

4. Connection & Support

- **Call or text a trusted friend or sponsor** who understands your healing path.

- **Join an online or in-person support group** to share and receive encouragement.

- **Use affirmations:** "I am safe. I am whole. This too shall pass."

5. Nourishment & Hydration

- Sip herbal teas such as chamomile, peppermint, or lavender.

- Eat a small, balanced snack with protein and healthy fats if hunger triggers cravings.

- Keep water nearby and stay hydrated throughout the day.

The 12-Week Cannabis Reduction Journey

A Path to Balance, Healing, and Renewal

Welcome to your sacred 12-week journey toward healing, balance, and transformation. Each week builds upon the last, weaving together gentle cannabis reduction, endocannabinoid support, dopamine regulation, spiritual practices, fear reduction techniques, community connection, dietary and supplement guidance, and empowering mantras. This plan honors your body, mind, and spirit, inviting you to walk with grace, awareness, and compassion every step of the way.

Week 0

Preparation Chapter — Creating Sacred Ground for the Journey

Before you begin your 12-week healing path, pause here to ground yourself in clarity, intention, and readiness.

1. Sacred Intention-Setting

Before any great transformation, there is a moment of commitment. Take time to reflect:

- Why are you choosing this path now?

- What do you hope to gain — emotionally, physically, spiritually?

- What does healing mean to you?

Suggested practices: Light a candle, write your intentions in a journal, and speak them aloud. Feel their resonance in your body.

2. Inventory & Reflection

Assess your current relationship with cannabis:

- How much do you use daily or weekly?

- What situations, emotions, or patterns trigger use?

- What unmet needs has cannabis been addressing? Ex. Depression, Trauma, Anxiety, Loneliness

_____

_____

_____

_____

_____

_____

_____

_____

_____

_____

_____

3. Creating a Healing Nest

Design your environment to support healing:

- Gather supplies: journal, teas, supplements, supportive books.

- Clear out triggers (paraphernalia, social connections that center cannabis).

- Set up a cozy, calming space for meditation and reflection.

4. Support & Accountability

Reach out to trusted people or a professional who can walk with you.

- Who can you call during hard moments? (see resources in index)

- Who will celebrate your milestones? List your supports below:

_____

_____

_____

_____

_____

_____

5. Embodied Readiness

Practice 3 days of gentle detox habits before starting:

- Hydrate well.

- Prioritize sleep.

- Eat nutrient-dense, whole foods.

- Try one daily mindfulness practice (5-minute breath awareness).

Mantra: *"I create the space for healing. I am ready. I am rooted. I am whole."*

12-Week Cannabis Titration Chart: A Gradual Path to Zero

Week	Target % of Original Daily Use	Daily Dose Example: If Starting at 3 grams/Day	Notes & Focus
Week 1	85–90%	2.5–2.7 grams	Begin gentle reduction. Introduce nervous system support + intention setting.
Week 2	75–80%	2.25–2.4 grams	Add dopamine-boosting nutrition. Support withdrawal symptoms.
Week 3	65–70%	2.0–2.1 grams	Practice grounding rituals and soothing cravings somatically.
Week 4	55–60%	1.65–1.8 grams	Increase spiritual practices and ECS-supportive foods.
Week 5	45–50%	1.35–1.5 grams	Build motivation, reframe identity beyond cannabis.
Week 6	35–40%	1.05–1.2 grams	Practice self-trust. Amplify joyful movement and connection.
Week 7	25–30%	0.75–0.9 grams	Deepen resilience. Release past stories held in the body.
Week 8	15–20%	0.45–0.6 grams	Begin envisioning a life beyond cannabis. Strengthen new habits.
Week 9	10–15%	0.3–0.45 grams	Microdose (if needed) or reduce to evening only. Trust inner guidance.
Week 10	5–10%	0.15–0.3 grams	Use spiritual tools during cravings. Activate future self.
Week 11	2–5%	0.05–0.15 grams	Final taper — may skip days or use 1–2 puffs if needed.
Week 12	0%	0 grams	Completion. Anchor new identity. Create cessation ritual.

How to Use This Chart:

- **Start with your current daily use** (e.g., 3 grams, 6 vape hits, 2 edibles, etc.).

- Multiply your use by the percentage for each week to get your **target dosage**.

- Use tools such as **pre-weighing**, **partial consumption**, or **alternating delivery methods** (e.g., dry herb vape with less material) to reduce quantity.

- If using a **vape or pipe**, use **measured hits** instead of whole sessions.

- Always listen to your body. Go slower if needed, but try not to reverse direction unless for safety

Week 1

Grounding & Nervous System Regulation

Begin this journey gently, laying a foundation of calm and presence as you initiate your cannabis taper.

Cannabis Reduction:

Start reducing to 85-90% ex. 2 grams a day. Practice mindful smoking—notice triggers without judgment.

Endocannabinoid Support:

Spend 10 minutes daily in grounding breath awareness and gentle movement. Incorporate moderate sun exposure.

Dopamine Regulation:

Include protein-rich foods at breakfast to support motivation. Try short bursts of aerobic activity.

Spiritual Practices:

Practice body scan meditation and grounding visualization. Tune into 432 Hz frequency for calm and connection.

Reducing Fear:

Engage in grounding breath awareness and gentle neck rolls. Affirm: "I am safe and steady."

Community Integration:

Reach out to a supportive friend or attend a group event.

Dietary & Supplements:

Start B-complex and omega-3 supplements. Focus on whole foods and hydration.

Mantra:

"I begin this journey with openness and strength."

Compassionate Reflection

Intention & Starting the Process

- What is calling me to make this change?

- Who am I becoming through this process?

- What fears arise as I begin, and how can I meet them with compassion?

Week 2

Supporting the Endocannabinoid System

Deepen your connection with your body's natural healing mechanisms.

Cannabis Reduction:

Reduce to 75-80% ex. 1.75 grams/day. Notice cravings and respond with breath.

Endocannabinoid Support:

Add walnuts or hemp seeds to meals. Practice 10 minutes of moderate stretching plus sun exposure daily.

Dopamine Regulation:

Snack on dark chocolate (70% or higher) in moderation. Include short aerobic bursts.

Spiritual Practices:

Begin morning gratitude journaling and loving-kindness meditation. Tune into 528 Hz frequency for healing.

Reducing Fear:

Practice gentle humming with neck and shoulder rolls. Affirm: "I am grounded and secure."

Community Integration:

Volunteer or help a neighbor. Attend a local event or workshop.

Dietary & Supplements:

Incorporate turmeric into cooking.

Mantra:

"I nurture my mind, body, and spirit with kindness."

Compassionate Reflection

Awareness of Habit & Pattern

- What moments or emotions most often trigger my desire to use cannabis?

- How have I used cannabis to cope, escape, or connect?

- What patterns am I ready to release?

Week 3

Dopamine Regulation & Healing Activation

Focus on stabilizing motivation and awakening resilience.

Cannabis Reduction:

Reduce to 65-70% ex. 1.5 grams/day. Practice mindful smoking and observe without judgment.

Endocannabinoid Support:

Add flaxseed or chia to meals. Spend mindful time outdoors.

Dopamine Regulation:

Eat tyrosine-rich foods like eggs, cheese, soy. Incorporate joyful movement like dance.

Spiritual Practices:

Practice full 15-minute meditation sessions. Connect with ancestors through prayer. Tune into 639 Hz frequency for heart opening.

Reducing Fear:

Use chanting or soft singing for 5 minutes. Use a weighted blanket for grounding. Affirm: "Peace begins within me."

Community Integration:

Host or participate in a small group. Share meaningful insights.

Dietary & Supplements:

Include leafy greens daily.

Mantra:

"Each day, I become more whole and free."

Compassionate Reflection

Grounding the Body

- What sensations live in my body when I feel a craving or stress?

- How do I feel after engaging in grounding practices like breathwork or movement?

- In what ways can I offer more care to my physical body?

Week 4

Healing Response & Nervous System Calm

Enhance nervous system regulation and emotional resilience.

Cannabis Reduction:

Reduce to 55-60% ex. 1 gram/day. Reflect weekly progress in your journal.

Endocannabinoid Support:

Add an evening walk in natural light. Practice mindful eating.

Dopamine Regulation:

Snack on tyrosine-rich foods like pumpkin seeds. Try 10 minutes of dance or free movement.

Spiritual Practices:

Silent meditation focusing on breath. Tend a plant or garden.

Reducing Fear:

Practice slow exhale breathing with humming. Walk barefoot on natural surfaces. Affirm: "Calm and strength flow through me."

Community Integration:

Join a new group or class. Reach out to a supportive person.

Dietary & Supplements:

Add anti-inflammatory spices like ginger and cinnamon.

Mantra:

"With calm and clarity, I face each moment."

Compassionate Reflection

Navigating the Emotional Landscape

- What emotions have surfaced more strongly since I began reducing cannabis?

- How do I typically respond to difficult feelings — and how would I like to respond instead?

- Where do I need more gentleness?

Week 5

Deepening Healing & Growth

Encourage growth through self-compassion and new experiences.

Cannabis Reduction:

Reduce to 45-50% ex. 0.75 grams/day. Practice craving delay: wait 10 minutes and breathe deeply when urges arise.

Endocannabinoid Support:

Add hemp protein or seeds. Try gentle swimming or water-based movement.

Dopamine Regulation:

Eat tyrosine-rich snacks like pumpkin seeds. Try a new physical activity for 20 minutes.

Spiritual Practices:

Visualization meditation focused on healing. Write a letter to an ancestor or future self.

Reducing Fear:

Slow rocking in a chair or hammock. Self-massage on neck and scalp. Affirm: "I am safe in my body."

Community Integration:

Join a new inspiring group or class. Reach out for support.

Dietary & Supplements:

Add ginger and cinnamon. Continue magnesium and omega-3 supplements.

Mantra:

"I am open to healing and growth in all forms."

Compassionate Reflection

Reclaiming Joy & Natural Dopamine

- What activities bring me genuine joy, without needing to alter my state?

- When do I feel most energized, inspired, or alive?

- What kind of joy do I want to invite more of into my life?

Week 6

Enhancing Endocannabinoid Support

Focus on nutrition and mindful movement.

Cannabis Reduction:

Reduce to 35-40% ex. 0.5 grams/day. Reflect on emotional triggers with self-compassion.

Endocannabinoid Support:

Practice 20 minutes mindful walking outdoors. Optional sauna or steam sessions.

Dopamine Regulation:

Add lean proteins like chicken or tofu. Engage in playful movement such as dancing or jumping rope.

Spiritual Practices:

Silent meditation on breath sensations. Tend a small garden or plant.

Reducing Fear:

Extended exhales with humming for 7 minutes. Ground by walking barefoot. Affirm: "Calm and strength flow through me."

Community Integration:

Volunteer in a helping role. Share personal insights with trusted groups.

Dietary & Supplements:

Include berries and nuts daily. Consider adaptogens like ashwagandha or rhodiola.

Mantra:

"With calm and clarity, I face each moment."

Compassionate Reflection

Embracing the Shadow

- What aspects of myself do I struggle to accept — and why?

- How can I practice loving these parts instead of rejecting them?

- What lessons are hidden in the discomfort I feel?

Week 7

Dopamine Balance & Motivation Renewal

Renew motivation through joyful activity and connection.

Cannabis Reduction:

Reduce to 25-30% ex. 0.25 grams/day or abstain if ready. Use distraction with hobbies or creative projects.

Endocannabinoid Support:

Add walnuts or pumpkin seeds. Practice 15 minutes restorative yoga.

Dopamine Regulation:

Snack on dark chocolate moderately. Include short cardio bursts like jogging or stairs.

Spiritual Practices:

Loving-kindness meditation focused on self and others. Light a candle and meditate on gratitude.

Reducing Fear:

Chant or sing mantras aloud. Use a weighted blanket before sleep. Affirm: "I am grounded, calm, and safe."

Community Integration:

Attend community events. Offer encouragement to others.

Dietary & Supplements:

Use turmeric and ginger regularly. Continue magnesium, omega-3, and B-complex.

Mantra:

"I honor my journey and my resilience."

Compassionate Reflection

Trusting the Process

- Where in my life have I already made powerful changes?

- What would it feel like to fully trust my body's healing intelligence?

- What does surrender mean to me right now?

Week 8

Envisioning a Life Beyond Cannabis

Embody your healing self with presence and gratitude.

Cannabis Reduction:

Reduce to 15-20% Abstain or use only CBD flower as needed. Reflect on progress and set intentions.

Endocannabinoid Support:

Add flaxseed or chia daily. Spend mindful time in nature.

Dopamine Regulation:

Eat tyrosine-rich foods like eggs, cheese, fish. Engage in playful or social physical activity.

Spiritual Practices:

Daily meditation on connection and presence. Perform practice of gratitude or blessing.

Reducing Fear:

Slow breath with humming for 10 minutes. Mindful barefoot walking. Affirm: "I am calm, centered, and whole."

Community Integration:

Host or co-host a group meditation. Deepen community bonds.

Dietary & Supplements:

Continue anti-inflammatory foods. Review supplements with provider.

Mantra:

"I move forward with peace and purpose."

Compassionate Reflection

Strengthening Inner Connection

- What wisdom is my body offering me today?

- How can I attune more deeply to my intuition?

- Who or what helps me return to my center?

Week 9

Nervous System Resilience

Build resilience to stress and deepen calm.

Cannabis Reduction:

Reduce to 10-25%. Maintain abstinence or use CBD as needed. Practice mindfulness during cravings.

Endocannabinoid Support:

Add 1 tbsp hemp seeds daily. Practice 20 minutes gentle Qi Gong or Tai Chi.

Dopamine Regulation:

Eat tyrosine-rich snacks like pumpkin seeds or cheese. Try interval training alternating fast/slow walking.

Spiritual Practices:

Morning gratitude meditation. Create vision board or symbolic artwork.

Reducing Fear:

Extended exhale breathing with humming for 10 minutes. Self-massage scalp and shoulders. Affirm: "I release fear and embrace calm."

Community Integration:

Volunteer for community projects. Deepen social connections with heartfelt conversation.

Dietary & Supplements:

Maintain anti-inflammatory diet with turmeric and berries. Add probiotics or fermented foods if tolerated.

Mantra:

"I embrace calm and clarity in every moment."

Compassionate Reflection

Integrating Mind, Body & Spirit

- How have I changed since Week 1?

- In what ways do I feel more aligned, clear, or connected?

- What practices help me integrate all parts of myself?

Week 10

Integrating Endocannabinoid Balance

Sustain balance through lifestyle integration.

Cannabis Reduction:

Reduce 5-10%. Full abstinence or occasional non-psychoactive use. Reflect on triggers and coping.

Endocannabinoid Support:

Add walnuts or flaxseed daily. Practice 15 minutes restorative yoga.

Dopamine Regulation:

Include lean protein. Engage in 20 minutes playful physical activity like dance or hiking.

Spiritual Practices:

Loving-kindness meditation focused on self and ancestors. Offer ritual or song of thanks.

Reducing Fear:

Deep belly breathing with vocal sighs. Use nature touchstone for grounding. Affirm: "I am fully supported."

Community Integration:

Attend group practice or wellness event. Offer service or insight.

Dietary & Supplements:

Maintain whole food anti-inflammatory diet. Review supplements with provider.

Mantra:

"I honor my healing and open to joy."

Compassionate Reflection

Nurturing Your Nervous System

- When do I feel most safe and regulated?

- What calms my breath, slows my thoughts, and softens my body?

- How can I prioritize nervous system care moving forward?

Week 11

Dopamine Sustenance & Community Integration

Sustain motivation and nurture social support.

Cannabis Reduction:

Reduce 2-5%. Continue abstinence. Celebrate milestones. Journal gratitude for your body's resilience.

Endocannabinoid Support:

Practice daily sun exposure and movement. Try 20 minutes forest bathing.

Dopamine Regulation:

Eat protein-rich breakfasts. Enjoy upbeat music with movement.

Spiritual Practices:

Practice 30 minutes silence meditation. Reflect on dreams or intuitive messages.

Reducing Fear:

Light neck massage with humming. Use butterfly hug or self-holding. Affirm: "I am safe, I am home in my body."

Community Integration:

Lead or co-lead a healing group or nature walk. Acknowledge supporters.

Dietary & Supplements:

Incorporate prebiotics and fermented foods. Stay hydrated with herbal teas.

Mantra:

"I am held in love, clarity, and balance.

Compassionate Reflection

Celebrating Growth

- What am I most proud of in this journey?

- What limiting beliefs have I released?

- What strengths have I uncovered or reclaimed?

Week 12

Celebration & Continued Healing

Complete this sacred passage with gratitude and vision.

Cannabis Reduction:

Celebrate full cessation or your personal goal. Set intentions for continued growth.

Endocannabinoid Support:

Spend time in nature with gratitude. Practice breathwork and movement daily.

Dopamine Regulation:

Enjoy nourishing foods. Engage in joyful activities that bring pleasure.

Spiritual Practices:

Create a ritual of closure and new beginnings. Meditate on your healing light.

Reducing Fear:

Practice long exhale breath with humming. Affirm: "I walk forward in peace and light."

Community Integration:

Celebrate with your community. Share your story to inspire others.

Dietary & Supplements:

Maintain a whole foods-based diet. Reflect on supplement needs with provider.

Mantra:

"My journey is infinite, sacred, and radiant."

Compassionate Reflection

Completion & Continuation

- What does completion mean to me — and what continues beyond this?

- What practices or behaviors do I want to carry with me?

- How will I honor and celebrate the path I've walked?

_____

_____

_____

_____

_____

_____

_____

_____

_____

_____

_____

_____

_____

_____

_____

_____

_____

_____

The Ever-Flowing Path

Completion, Celebration & What Comes Next

As you arrive at the closing of this sacred 12-week journey, know this: it is not an end, but a transformation. A spiral opening. A return to yourself, more radiant and rooted than before. You have crossed a threshold — from reliance to sovereignty, from confusion to clarity, from numbness to presence. What you hold now is not just freedom from cannabis — it is freedom to embody your light more fully.

This moment of completion deserves celebration. Not as a finish line, but as a sacred recognition: **You did it. You showed up. You stayed with yourself. You healed.**

You have walked through cravings like wildfire and chosen the cool river of your breath. You've listened when your body whispered for rest. You've remembered your rhythm, tended the fire of intention, and restored the flow of your sacred neurobiology. You've come home.

Tending the Embers: A Living Practice

Healing is not a static state. It is a living relationship — with your body, your mind, your spirit, and the ever-shifting environment around you. What you've learned over these 12 weeks is not just how to let go of a substance — it's how to live with reverence, presence, and gentleness.

The **Firekeeper** within you — your prefrontal cortex — still watches over your choices. Tend this flame with intention.

Morning routines, evening reflection, mindful decisions — these are the sparks that keep your clarity glowing.

The **Emotional Guardian** — your amygdala — still responds to stress and fear. Honor its vigilance. Breathe into tension. Let calmness wrap around you like sacred smoke. Your nervous system remembers the way home.

The **Keepers Of Balance** — your endocannabinoid system and hippocampus — continues to shape your emotional landscapes. Feed this emotional current with nature, connection, and nourishment. This is your garden now — and you are the tender of its balance.

The **Breath of Renewal** — your dopamine system — will keep inviting you to create, connect, and move with joyful purpose. Let your motivation be sacred. Play, dance, sing. Let life be delicious again, without needing to be dulled or delayed.

Honoring Your Completion: A Celebration of Renewal

You may wish to mark this moment with a **completion celebration** — a way of honoring your soul's commitment and the sacred work you've done. Some possibilities:

- **Write a letter** to your past self, the one who began this journey. Offer them gratitude, compassion, and love.

- **Create a small space** with symbols of your transformation — a candle, a feather, a river stone, a photograph of your favorite place in nature.

- **Invite trusted friends or guides** into a circle of reflection. Speak your truth. Be witnessed.

- **Plant something** — a flower, a tree, an herb. Let your healing grow roots in the earth.

- **Dance under the stars**. Let your body say what words cannot.

Let this ritual not just close the circle but open the next one.

What Comes Next: Integrating and Expanding

Now that cannabis no longer defines your rhythm, ask yourself: *What do I truly want to feel, to create, to become?* The energy you once gave to self-soothing can now be redirected toward your sacred work, your community, your joy.

Some next steps you might explore:

- **Continue spiritual expansion** through meditation, prayer, dreamwork, or frequency-based healing.

- **Deepen relationships** with kindred spirits — those who honor your growth and uplift your path.

- **Engage your gifts** — write, teach, create, speak, offer healing. The world needs your medicine.

- **Revisit this guide** as a living text — update your routines, retune your nervous system, return when needed.

- **Support others** who are beginning their own healing journey. You are now a wisdom bearer. A guide.

Integration Beyond 12 Weeks — Walking the Ever-Flowing Path

Your 12-week journey has been a sacred spiral inward and upward. As you step beyond this initial container, integration becomes your daily rhythm — a weaving of new neural pathways, spiritual insights, and lifestyle choices into your lived reality. This phase is not about perfection; it's about embodied presence, steady tending, and joyful expansion.

1. Anchoring Daily Practices (Choose 3–5 to begin)

Consistency supports your nervous system and your spirit. Let your rituals become sacred punctuation marks in your day.

Suggested Daily Practices:

- Morning grounding (breathwork, intention setting, movement)

- Midday check-in: "What do I need right now?"

- Evening wind-down (journaling, herbal tea, gentle music)

- Nourishing meals with intention and presence

- Gratitude list (3 things before bed)

Optional Weekly Additions:

- Digital detox day

- Creative play (art, dance, writing)

- Volunteer or community engagement

2. Monthly Self-Check Reflection

Once a month, create time to reflect on these guiding questions:

- Where am I feeling most alive right now?

- What's shifting in my emotions, thoughts, or body?

- Are there new challenges, and how am I supporting myself?

- What support (inner or outer) do I need at this stage of healing?

- What am I celebrating in myself this month?

Create a spiritual practice around this — light a candle, journal in nature, speak aloud to your guides, or create a collage.

3. Stay Rooted in Support & Community

Healing is sustained in connection. Whether through a trusted friend, a therapist, a support group, or a spiritual community, choose people and spaces that uplift, ground, and mirror your growth.

Ideas for Continued Support:

- Join or create a cannabis-free circle or conscious living group

- Attend or facilitate healing circles, meditations, or somatic movement classes

- Stay in regular touch with 1–2 accountability partners

- Practice compassionate sharing — express your truth and allow others to do the same

4. Keep Listening to Your Body

Your body is your greatest teacher. Cravings, fatigue, tension, and joy are all communications. Let your body lead. Notice changes in:

- Sleep rhythms

- Energy levels

- Libido and pleasure

- Appetite and digestion

- Sensory sensitivity (sound, light, taste, etc.)

Respond by asking:

"What does this part of me need?" "What feels safe and nourishing in this moment?"

5. Explore New Layers of Joy, Purpose, and Creativity

Now is the time to expand into what your soul came here to do. With cannabis no longer numbing or distorting your inner compass, clarity and creative energy naturally rise.

Try asking yourself:

- What passions or projects have I been postponing?

- What creative expressions want to emerge now?

- What does it mean to live in alignment with my truth?

You may feel called to write, garden, sing, build, dance, speak, mentor, or rest deeply. All are sacred.

6. Continue Co-Creating with the Sacred

Let your healing path evolve into a living relationship with spirit, the earth, and your higher self.

Ongoing spiritual practices might include:

- Nature communion and ancestral honoring

- Working with elements (earth, fire, water, air, ether)

- Dialoguing with higher guidance

- Dreamwork, lucid dreaming, or astral exploration

- Offering your healing journey in service to others

Final Blessing

Your Infinite Light

You are not the same being who began this journey. You are wiser, more embodied, more attuned to your truth.

The path does not end. It spirals ever outward. Your presence is the medicine. Your joy is the transmission. Your life — unfolding in its own sacred time — is a gift to this Earth.

So breathe, beloved. Smile gently. Walk on in grace.

The world awaits the gifts only you can give.

Resource Appendix

A Treasure Chest for Your Healing Journey

This appendix gathers recommended books, websites, apps, supplements, and community resources to support your path beyond the 12 weeks.

Books

- *The Body Keeps the Score* by Bessel van der Kolk — Trauma and healing through body awareness

- *The Mindful Way Through Addiction* by Sarah Bowen — Mindfulness-based relapse prevention

- *Healing with Whole Foods* by Paul Pitchford — Nutrition and nourishment for body and mind

Websites & Online Communities

- SMART Recovery (smartrecovery.org) — Science-based addiction support

- Marijuana Anonymous (marijuana-anonymous.org)- Cannabis dependency support groups

- Reddit r/leaves - Support for cannabis cessation

Apps for Mindfulness and Support

- Insight Timer - Guided meditations and community groups

- Headspace or Calm - Daily mindfulness and sleep support

- MyFitnessPal - Track nutrition and hydration

- Recovery Record - Support for addiction recovery journaling

Supplements & Nutrition

- Omega-3 fatty acids (flaxseed oil, fish oil) for endocannabi-noid system support

- Magnesium glycinate for nervous system calming

- L-tyrosine rich foods to support dopamine pathways (eggs, fish, cheese)

- Vitamin D and B-complex for mood regulation and energy

*Consult your healthcare provider before beginning any supplement regimen.

Local & Virtual Support Options

- Licensed therapists specializing in trauma and addiction recovery

- Community healing circles, yoga studios, or meditation centers

- Online peer support groups, forums, and webinars

- Workshops on nervous system regulation, breathwork, or somatic therapy

About the Author

 **Nichole Sloan (Nickie)** is a licensed clinical social worker, trauma-informed therapist, and longtime practitioner of mindfulness and compassion-based healing. For over two decades, she has walked alongside others in their journeys toward wholeness, weaving together deep listening, emotional attunement, and somatic presence to create spaces where transformation can unfold.

With a background in both clinical mental health and contemplative practices, Nickie's work bridges science and soul. She is a devoted advocate for nervous system healing, vibrational awareness, and the reclamation of inner sovereignty. Her writings and teachings explore the intersection of emotional resilience, energetic integrity, and collective liberation.

Nickie lives in Georgia, where she tends to her garden, cares for animals and listens deeply to the rhythms of nature. She enjoys traveling, creating art, contemplative practices and engaging in community care and advocacy. She believes that healing is not a destination but a remembering of one's own wisdom and power.

www.ingramcontent.com/pod-product-compliance
Lightning Source LLC
Chambersburg PA
CBHW071537120626
46550CB00006B/2485

www.ingramcontent.com/pod-product-compliance
Lightning Source LLC
Chambersburg PA
CBHW071537120626
46550CB00006B/2485